Melancholia

Melancholia

Poems by

Alan Balter

Cover design by Shay Culligan

ISBN: 978-1-952326-30-1

Kelsay Books
502 South 1040 East, A-119
American Fork, Utah, 84003

To Barbara

The Lake

waters, the color of jade
slide ashore in liquid whispers
to wet the dune grass standing like sentinels
in a vast and verdant brigade

as a boy, I splashed in the shallows
to catch silver minnows in a frayed,
cotton cloth, and I showed them to a girl
whose eyes were the color of cornflowers

and when we were still young and fresh,
we ran, hand in hand, into the cold surf
where we warmed each other and spoke
of all the sweet things that life would bring us

and now, after the ebb and flow of thousands of tides,
I sit onshore of the great lake and reflect
upon the wonders of the waters and the woman
I love as I love my life

Acknowledgments

Western Quarterly Magazine: "Snowflakes"

Love Poetry Magazine: "Rose"

Love Poetry Magazine: "One More Summer"
    (now And I was Young Again)

Better Than Starbucks Magazine: "Joy of the Game"

Better After Fifty Magazine: "You Were Once My Mother"

New York Literary Magazine: "When Will It End?"

Contents

Snowflakes

snowflakes swirling through the trees
cool my lips and tongue
transient as my memories
of times when I was young

once I dashed around the bases
fleet afoot and agile
now confined to lesser places
I'm ancient, stiff and fragile

I dream of playing but one more time
Sam and Howie and me
just one more game in our prime
how joyous it would be

in my dream there is no sorrow
legs loosen and grow stronger
dawn begins a sweet tomorrow
and snowflakes last much longer

Mother Wants to Die

Bobby Lee raped five women and slashed them to the bone,
and while his last meal cooled greasy on a tin plate,
a portly priest held him close and listened:

"I have no joy, no comfort, no hope, and I'd rather be dead,
so let their poison flow that I might rest, maybe in peace,"
and we did.

Mother wants to die too, but no one listens,
so she rocks in her chair day after day
and stares through dead eyes at pictures
of loved ones, long forgotten, on the wall.

and never smiles or laughs or has any hope
and takes nourishment through a feeding tube
and has yet another stroke that renders her still
and lies in stench until someone changes her diapers
and waits for her husband, twenty years dead, to visit
and gags on mind numbing drugs forced upon her
and thinks she's in a prison
and says "help me" a thousand times over,
and we don't

why is it, I wonder, that we help murderers and rapists find peace,
but we won't do the same for our sweet mothers?

And I Was Young Again

there was a summer place in Michigan
nestled onshore of the big lake
where I walked along the soft sand beach
among seagulls pecking at perch

green breakers laced with foam rolled ashore
while the sun burned quick on my face and back,
then under a leafy canopy, I picked wildflowers,
still damp with dew, for Maggie

the forest thinned into a stretch of rolling hills
dotted by decrepit sawmills from an earlier time
and loggers' cabins rife with moss and fungus
and spiders spinning their sticky webs

then Maggie, with her sweet country mouth and
scent of lavender showed me her body
and we made slow love under the northern sky
shimmering with green and purple

if only I could return to that summer place
where everything near me seemed to rhyme,
and cool breezes freshened the night air
punctuated by fireflies in crazy abundance,
and I was young again

Great Grandpa's Shoes

they came in darkness and ripped us from our beds to cattle cars so
crammed we couldn't sit, and our people prayed and vomited and
shit before the lucky ones died where they stood

at last, the doors creaked open to savage men and menacing
shepherd dogs with yellow fangs dripping froth and snapping and
snarling as if rabies had infested their dim, canine brains

the smell of burnt flesh befouled the air while they stripped us
naked and shaved our heads and tattooed our forearms with black
numbers to remind us they had stolen our names

they tore our wives away to rape and ravage, and our children too,
quivering in terror, and gave us black and white striped clothes of
coarse cloth at once impotent against the bitter cold

a corps of maniacs mined our teeth for gold, then castrated and
sterilized us and submerged us in icy waters, in their insane quest
for a superior race of teutonic monsters

in barracks with buckets for toilets and no water to wash, three
skeletal men shared a straw filled mattress, and together we starved
and stunk, and stiffened before the dawn

the shoes of the old and infirm were strewn in piles before they
herded us to shower under spigots spewing poison gas, leaving us
to claw at the metal doors until our fingers bled, and we were
incinerated and stacked in mass graves, up to six thousand
souls a day

a million people with somber faces and hushed voices walk the dimly lit halls of the museum each year to see the shoes on display, and some of them will never forget, because a pair belonged to Great Grandpa.

Anybody Home?

Jimmy and his mates stormed a beach
streaked with blood red sand
unsure whether to curse or pray,
he fell to his knees among severed limbs
and intestines, still steaming

back home, Jimmy slept in a cardboard box
that once housed a Maytag fridge
only to suffer night sweats and flashbacks
of empty eye sockets teeming with maggots

with his purple heart, paranoia, and one pair of socks
Jimmy took his breakfast under the overpass
a couple of pills, whatever the hell they were
washed down by three ounces of yesterday's wine

he toiled with a tin cup on a crowded corner
among people who looked away from his
once handsome face, and at dusk he tallied
his take home pay, ten quarters and a few dollars

he spent his earnings at the liquor store
on what he needed the most
then shared a swig with each of his mates
in a futile attempt to purge the night horrors

Jimmy died yesterday in his room for one
from an overdose of antifreeze that made his brain swell
Russell grabbed his coat, and Thomas took his socks
and a guy named Johnny moved into the box

Imagine

imagine a mansion atop a hill
amid weeping willow trees
where nowhere is there an alley found
or a tired old man peddling rags and old iron

a three story estate with a wrought iron gate
and a heated saltwater pool
but nowhere is there a dusty yard
to play red rover or hide and seek

six bedrooms each with bath en suite
with marble tile and golden faucets
but nowhere a place for the boys to strut
their stuff and tease the girls a while

oil paintings hang in splendid array
over lush carpets warming the floors
but echoes of emptiness bounce from the walls
because no children come inside

imagine aging in this mansion so fine
alone and never to roam
in your vast and vacant vertical shrine
teeming with things, yet barren

Queer Billy Burnside

Billy Burnside lived with his three older sisters
a kind and gentle boy who never stepped on ants
he went to school each day and made the honor roll
among classmates who were cruel as winter

Billy didn't play sports; he found them much too rough
instead he fashioned clay sculptures of super heroes
and wrote sonnets for friends who lived in his head
but would never know him

the other guys didn't like his style so after school one day
they tied him with rough ropes to a gnarly black oak tree
where hairy caterpillars and fat, brown worms
crawled over his shoes

they left him alone and went off to play their games
until just before the sun went down when they returned
to call him a sissy boy and a fruit and taunt him
for wetting his corduroy knickers

a policeman came to free him and walk him home
this kind and gentle boy who didn't have much to say
he stumbled up the stairs and sat atop his bed
where queer Billy Burnside put a bullet through his head

Once Again

a trillion life forms descended to Earth
spreading alien venom through the species
that turned coal black and petrified
as if stony substances

so it was across many millennia
silent, save for the rush of wind and water
and the stones eroded to dust
and the land was bleak and barren

then upon a windswept plain
a place bathed by gentle rains and rays
a red bloom stretched toward the sun
a flower, once again a flower

what was but one multiplied to many
and bees flitted among them to sip their nectar
and crawling things sucked the sap
of trees grown thick and tall

the rivers filled anew with swimming things
so profuse they made slapping sounds upon the surface
and amphibia crept from wet to dry to take the sun
with gibbons and silverback gorillas

through the forests, now lush and verdant
sounds of life emanated
humming across the mountain ranges
we're coming, once again we're coming

My Brother Tommy

on Mom's bad days when she's depressed
she'll down eight or ten shots of vodka
or scotch or whatever is left over
and a couple of beers for chasers

like a butcher with a keen blade
she daily dissects the future of my fetal brother
who is only about three inches long
but already has a face

it's seven years later, and your name is Tommy
a sweet little guy with a hole in your heart
who is so slow to learn and doesn't see very well
yet still reaches out for his mommy

you find your place on the short bus over there
and ride to school with little people as damaged as you
your teacher sends you home with books I read aloud
while we wait once again for the pizza delivery man

I had a chance to go east for college
with an academic scholarship to Yale
but I'll be staying home when the ivy turns
because who will care for Tommy?

Rose and Me

I built our cabin in a distant place
on a hill amidst a stand of white pines
near pristine lake waters lapping a sandy shore
where Rose and I walked in the fall

we hiked the trails with our dear mutt Duke
through trees infused with fiery orange and red
softened by the season's smear of ink
purple, pink, and muted yellow

Rose wore jeans and a woolen sweater
or sometimes an old pea coat when the hawk flew.
back at the cabin, we'd have a glass of wine
and sing every folk song we ever knew

for dessert, there was warm apple pie
smothered with molten vanilla ice cream
and when the barn owls hooted in nocturnal chorus
Rose and I made love by the fire

then a putrid presence sneaked into the cabin
and tore into her like a jagged rip saw
tearful whimpers grew to wretched shrieks
as chemicals poisoned her to the marrow

each day I watched her drift away
dulled by massive doses of morphine.
when she finally slept, I gathered her hair
and spilt some salty water

near the surf, we walked upon cool sand
and spoke of everything we'd ever planned
but now it's silent save a low pitched moan
for to the cabin in the fall, I go alone

Depression

a dismal dawn, dreary and wet
ushers in yet another day of
hollow, hopeless hours
on the lip of oblivion

a murky space is where I live
where the air reeks of rot
and dry heaves spew bloody clots
that taste sour, like bile

fitful sleep is my escape
from the pounding of my pulse
still, I dream of a green eyed boy
who once played in the sun

come sup with me, a buffet for two
at once simple and severe
an appetizer of mind altering drugs
and a main course of despair

curled into a fetal position
with my knees drawn to my chest
am I living or am I dead
and which one is second best?

Fuer Elise Forever

on a promising Sunday in the spring when the
hint of lilac leaked through the windows and
the smell of old people leaked out, my aunts and uncles
gathered to hear me spin a few tunes on the spinet

like many other flashes, I flared out early and
other kids, mostly studious types with briefcases,
passed me by while I got stuck on Fuer Elise forever
like a goddamned ice cream truck

my repertoire consisted of silly little songs with
a few staccatos and grace notes and a couple
fortissimos not nearly bold enough to muffle
the jubilant sounds of the ballgame
at the schoolyard down the street

a girl with a pony tail and short shorts
came to watch me play and would have
waited around for me to take her for a
chocolate soda after the game
instead of listening to me play an etude on the cracks

so I'll trade you one spinet for a pair of spiked shoes
and practicing scales for roaming free in left field
and a sixty minute lesson for the split second that
the ball nestles, soft and sure, in my hands

Dream with Me

on a planet a million light years away
where the air is warm and pure
four moons, each pastel in color
spread soft night light across the land

two golden suns and sweet tasting rain
nourish flora in abundance
so a riot of color adorns each day
like a tapestry in a house of royals

otters play in fresh water seas
with baby seals who swim unafraid
and white tailed fawns eat succulent plants
in fuchsia forests free of hunters

the people differ in color too
maroon skinned, orange, and blue
their children swim together in pools
and come to love each other

they go to school happy each day
to learn what is true and false
never crouching in dusty cloak closets
at the sound of bullets whizzing

so come with me to this world afar
we can be there in barely a minute
just close your eyes and share my dreams
still filled with horror and primal screams

The Hunter

the hunter slinks from the deck of his ship
to sneak up on an infant and crush his skull
he murders one whose essence colors the snow
with a mixture of bright blood and brains

who is this vicious predator
but an author of obscenity without an editor
who peels pelts from pups still breathing
then clubs the life from his brothers?

he's known as a "sealer" in the trade
a truly brave guy who stalks dreaded,
man eating, bundles of fur
who weigh twelve pounds and bark

he hauls still babies back to the ship
knowing three or four will make a fur coat
to warm a lady of substantial means
and her insubstantial soul

so here's to you vile hunter man
a coward with a goddamn sledge
keep sailing your ship to wherever you're bound
until a cyclone blows you to hell

Old Lady Lintz

Mrs. Lintz was an old lady, all wrinkled and stooped
who lived alone with sepia photos of her dead husband
on the walls and other antiques that she dusted daily
and a Steinway piano she had tuned every year for no one to play

her apartment faced the yard where we had our ball games
after school, and when we made too much noise, she cursed
in a language we didn't know and threw hot water on us

once every week she walked to the grocery to buy whatever
she ate, and one rainy day she slipped and fell on the slick concrete
where blood from her nose and brow dripped onto a bag of
oranges, a quarter pound of salami, and a sliced rye bread,
without seeds

her arms and legs flailed all about as she struggled
to get up, and soon she panicked and began to weep and wail
until I happened by and offered my hand

"Thank you Sonny," she said, as I helped her home
where mom was worried because it was almost dark;
we brought Mrs. Lintz in to attend to her face,
and after some rest and a salami sandwich, she smiled

mom checked up on her almost daily after that
and sat with her for tea and cakes in her parlor
and drove her to the doctor when she was feeling ill
and brought her warm blankets to ease the chill

no one noticed when Mrs. Lintz died,
until we found a note on the pillow by her side
"There's money for my cremation in my blue backpack,
and buy some bats and balls for the boys out back"

He Made Every Game

it was a nasty day, cold and misty, so most of the fans left by the third inning. He stayed though, leaning on the trunk of a sugar maple and pulling on a Chesterfield.

the other guys, all clad in fancy uniforms and cocky, had men on first and second in the top of the ninth with one out.

a double play would mean the championship, free beers and brats later on at Big Buster's Bar and Grill, and a story to tell my grandchildren when I was too old to walk.

a grounder, hard and low, twisted toward me. I snatched it ankle high, stepped on third, and tossed a dart, three feet high and whizzing, to first, nailing the runner by half a step, maybe less.

he pumped a fist, and a smile played around his lips. No further accolades were needed, because he was hard against seventy, and he still made every game.

he was my dad, and I miss him. every day I miss him.

On Some Tuesdays in the Spring

Sonny Johnson lived under Highway 95
sharing space with feral cats and vermin
'til they moved his blanket to the county jail
because the Man said he murdered Mary McFale

he faced the court with empty pockets
next to a pale faced public defender who didn't give a damn
a jury found him guilty in less than three hours
and sentenced him to die on a Tuesday in the spring

fatty pork and greens cooled on a tin plate
as a portly priest sanctified Sonny's soul
no stays of execution were offered up to save him
from being discarded like a mound of yesterday's trash

they bound him to the chair, "Old Sparky," they called it
and fastened electrodes to his limbs and head
beads of sweat on Sonny's forehead glistened
"ain't done the deed; how come y'all don't listen?"

the lights in the cell block flickered
and Sonny convulsed hard against the leather
and smoke curled from his head
and his blood bubbled and boiled
and his eyeballs melted and popped from their sockets
and his organs fried to well done
and his bladder leaked hot urine
and his body was barely cool
before they put him in the ground

Sonny's fate is justified in some holy books
that tell us "an eye for an eye" is the way
but does anyone care how many men are taken
with the chilling chance we were mistaken
on some Tuesdays in the spring

You Still Know Me

once they would have called you "feeble minded"
or "senile," but now they say you're "demented"
not that it matters to me my friend,
because I call you Michael

the nurses say you don't know me
but when I hold your quaking hand in mine
and a crooked smile plays around your lips
I know they're mistaken

not long ago we played our games
between sugar maple trees and a red brick building
where they warehoused sheets of metal for some war
instead of once brilliant men

and the day after, we went to college
where we learned the law yet still found time
to write poetry for pretty coeds with blond hair
and full lips who loved us in your rusty Studebaker

then somehow, it became today and I've come to
visit you, as I will tomorrow, and your eyes will
brighten because you still know me
my good and dear friend Michael

When Will it End?

Jacob was Black or African-American if you'd rather
his mother was a teacher, and his father welded steel
they lived in a brick bungalow on the south side of town
where punks and pimps prevailed

on Friday nights in the fall, people came to see
Jacob play, and he won a scholarship to a college
out west unlike a score of his classmates who ran
with the gangs and had precious few birthdays

he flew home to rest and enjoy his spring break
and to call pretty Mary who lived a few blocks north
the cabbie dropped him off at his front steps
just two tough yards short of a first down

a group of gangsters flashed some signs
to which Jacob had no response
in their vacant heads, they assumed he was a rival
to be slaughtered like a mangy dog on the prowl

blood seeped from his chest and spilled from his mouth
as Jacob's life ended on that warm night in April
Mom screamed,"Sweet Jesus, they took my son!"
while Dad suffered silently and polished his gun

In the Lateness of the Hour

the patter of the rain on the roof quiets
just as a dusty ray of sunlight filters through a
window pane and lands on a girl with silken skin
and eyes the color of the sky on a clear day in May

in the attic where termites feast on two by fours
and mice skitter among dust balls in the corners,
we have a fine luncheon of soda bread, marmalade
and sweet tea

then off to travel to a faraway land of wonders
where Black and Brown children start school
with an even chance

and nuclear bombs are buried deep in the desert so
people looking heavenward see the cold twinkle of stars
instead of missiles and hot mushrooms

and cars run on hydrogen gas to cleanse
the air, now sweet and pure, for people
whose charcoal tainted lungs, once hard with cancer,
soften and fade to pink

and street people come out from under the
viaducts to feel the sun on their faces
and to wash themselves clean in homes
with hot water and walls

and great coral reefs are ablaze with color and teeming
with damselfish and sea horses and blue striped snapper
instead of plastic

and then, the girl in the attic whose
sallow skin has thickened with malignancy
looks at me through black eyes as the ray of
sunlight fades in the lateness of the hour

No Cigars

Maggie and I were young and just married
so we made a baby who was coming in the fall
a cradle and dresser awaited this new person
who would be Caroline or Teddy

then came September and our babe was on the way
at the birthing place across town
where other men were pacing that dawn
before passing around cigars with blue or pink bands

I fell asleep on a green leather sofa
dreaming of a pretty girl graceful at the barre
then of a boy, tall and slender, with hair to his shoulders
standing across the yard pitching a curve ball

a gray haired nurse awakened me and
wrapped me in ample arms; gentle in her manner,
her name was Margaret, and she told me
that our little girl was born quiet and still

Caroline never gave a lusty cry
or took a first breath or suckled at Maggie's breast
so with empty arms that night in the fall
I flushed all my cigars

Lost

once I had a Lionel train
and a pair of hard toe hockey skates
a Duncan yoyo and a fielder's mitt
and my youth

and later I had an eight track of Dylan tunes
and a picture of the first girl I kissed
a set of keys to my blue and white '55 Chevy
and my summers

and then there was my fraternity pin
and a copy of *Catcher in the Rye*
my fake leather briefcase stuffed with irrelevance
and my grandparents

and a baseball I caught off Ernie's bat
next to my well-worn Playboy magazines
a silken sweater I brought home from Spain
and my way

the first love poem I ever wrote
and the sad novel I almost finished
so many classrooms filled with young people
and my friends

maybe they're all in a quiet place
on a slope near a mountain stream gurgling
waiting for me to find them again
or maybe they're lost forever

Finis

we sat in rows of pockmarked desks
struggling with our half written poems
about teenaged angst, lost love, and hopes
when the door burst open to filth

he leveled his killing machine at Mrs. Barnes
and shot a stream of lead that ripped open her chest
before she fell to the floor and her life blood drained
from her body, still twitching though already dead

he aimed anew and mowed down my friends
whose screams will echo forever in my head
and some slid under their desks in futile efforts to hide
while others mouthed useless prayers

seventeen beautiful young people died that day
and still we wait for someone to wash away
the lingering filth who would massacre us yet again
at places we're supposed to be safe

at today's funeral, there will be
another set of parents with red eyes
whose hearts will erode just a little bit more
every day of their lives because their child
will never get a day older

back in English class I find my poem
as crumpled and unfinished as my friends

Goddamn his fucking eyes.

About the Author

Alan Balter was born in Chicago and attended the Chicago Public Schools. He matriculated at the University of Illinois in Urbana in 1956 and earned a Bachelor's Degree in Psychology (1960) and a Master's Degree in Special Education (1962). Alan taught adolescents with developmental delays at Niles Township High School West for two years before returning to the University of Illinois and completing a Ph.D. in Special Education in 1968. While completing his degree, he taught undergraduate courses at the University of Illinois.

He worked as the Director of Secondary Special Education Services in Skokie, Illinois (Niles Township High Schools) before joining the faculty in the Special Education Department at Chicago State University. There, over a tenure of 32 years, he prepared teachers for children and adolescents with developmental delays, learning disabilities, and emotional disorders.

Dr. Balter has published two nonfiction books: Divided Apple: A Story about Teaching in Chicago and Learning Disabilities: A Book for Parents, both with Kendall-Hunt publishers. He has also published two novels: Holden and Me (Rockway Press), for which he received their international fiction award in 2006 and Different Ways of Being (Linkville Press). His essay, "Cruel and Unusual Endings," about physician-assisted suicide, appeared in the Op-Ed section of the Chicago Tribune in 2000.

Dr. Balter and his wife Barbara, also a retired teacher, live in Northbrook, Illinois. They enjoy extensive travel and 14 grandchildren.